The RAUCOUS ROYALS

TEST YOUR ROYAL WITS: CRACK CODES, SOLVE MYSTERIES, and DEDUCE which ROYAL RUMORS are TRUE.

Carlyn Beccia

To the most
Royal Gillian
— Carly Beccia
2009

HOUGHTON MIFFLIN COMPANY
BOSTON 2008

To my parents, Nancy and Joe,

who supported me through years of raucous misbehaving.

"History is a Distillation of Rumors."
— Carlyle, 1795–1881,
Scottish essayist, satirist, and historian

Borders, badges, and symbols used in this book are loosely related to the royalty depicted. For example, Anne Boleyn's royal badge was a falcon holding a scepter (page 22). Anne's daughter, Elizabeth I, later also adopted the falcon holding a scepter as her badge, and this badge can be seen on the borders of Elizabeth's page (page 38–39). Louis XIV adopted the sun as his symbol, seen above the doorway on page 43.

www.houghtonmifflinbooks.com

The text of this book is set in 14-point Perpetua.
The illustrations are digital art.

Library of Congress Cataloging-in-Publication Data is on file.

ISBN-13: 978-0-618-89130-6

Manufactured in China
WKT 10 9 8 7 6 5 4 3 2 1

Dear Reader,

Once a rumor is born, it never truly dies. Before television, tabloid magazines, and the Internet, rumors about royalty were started by clever jingles, silly cartoons, small books called pamphlets, and simple word of mouth. These rumors have survived more than five hundred years, and that's an awfully long time of "have you heard the one about . . . ?"

Some of these rumors are true. Some of them are false. And with some of them, we will never know. But all of these rumors are told to you in secret.

Please don't repeat them.

Sincerely,

The Author

Are These Rumors True or False?

King Richard III murdered his nephews.

pp. 10–14

Queen Anne Boleyn had six fingers.

pp. 21–24

Mary Queen of Scots plotted to assassinate her cousin Queen Elizabeth.

pp. 27–35

1431–1476   1452–1485   1491–1547   1501/1507–1536   1515–1557   1542–1587   1533–1603

Prince Dracula was a real vampire.

pp. 6–9

King Henry VIII was so fat that his servants had to carry him.

pp. 15–18

Queen Anne of Cleves looked like a horse.

pp. 25–26

Queen Elizabeth was afraid of mic

pp. 36–39

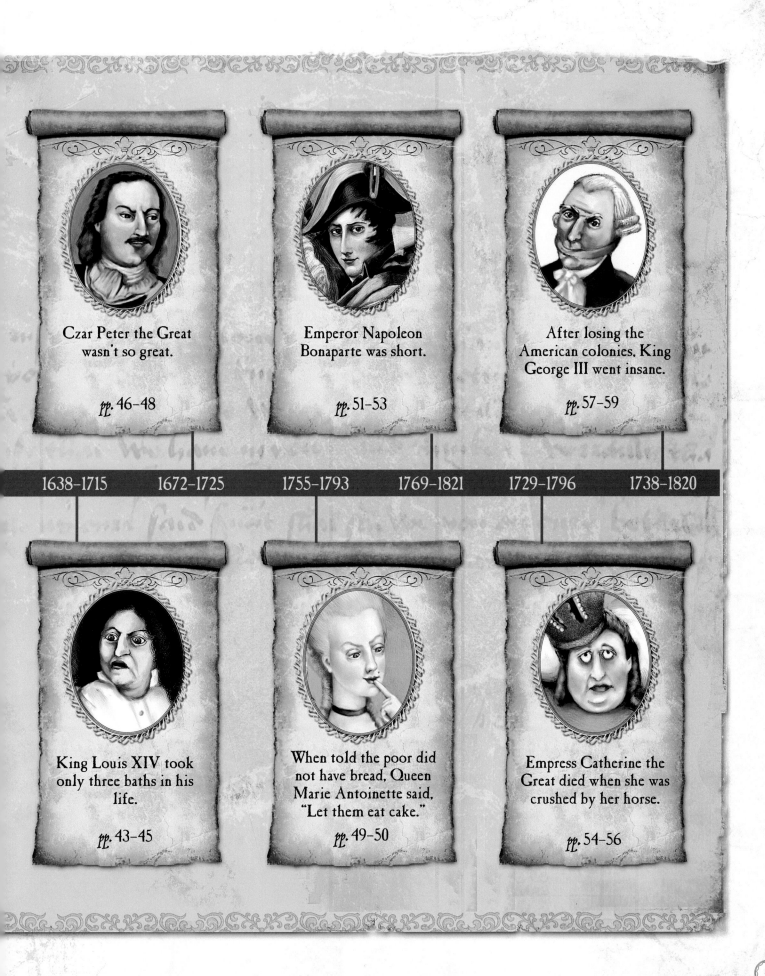

Czar Peter the Great wasn't so great.

pp. 46–48

Emperor Napoleon Bonaparte was short.

pp. 51–53

After losing the American colonies, King George III went insane.

pp. 57–59

1638–1715 1672–1725 1755–1793 1769–1821 1729–1796 1738–1820

King Louis XIV took only three baths in his life.

pp. 43–45

When told the poor did not have bread, Queen Marie Antoinette said, "Let them eat cake."

pp. 49–50

Empress Catherine the Great died when she was crushed by her horse.

pp. 54–56

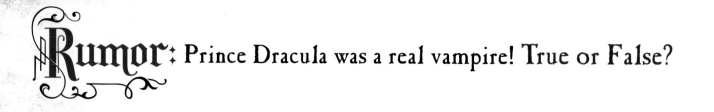

VLAD THE IMPALER

Vampires are scary stuff. They suck your blood. They turn into bats. And they are hard to get rid of without eating a hefty dose of garlic. In 1890, an Irish writer named Bram Stoker began researching vampire legends for a Gothic horror novel that he was writing. The name of Stoker's vampire was Count Wampyr. But during his research, Stoker came across the name of a fifteenth-century Wallachian prince called Vlad Dracula. Stoker thought *Dracula* sounded like a much scarier name for a vampire than *Wampyr*. What do you think? Count Wampyr or Count Dracula? Seems like no contest. If Stoker borrowed the name of Dracula for his story, are other details in his novel true? Was Dracula a real-life vampire baddie who lived in Wallachia (today Romania) more than five hundred years ago?

Turn the page to find out,
IF YOU DARE...

PRINCE OF ROMANIA, 1431 ~ 1476

Answer: UNCONFIRMED

The real story of Dracula is more horrible than any blood-sucking vampire tale. Here is the slightly less scary version. You have been warned!

The Real Prince of Darkness

In Romanian, *dracula* means "son of the dragon" or "son of the devil." Son of the devil, son of the dragon—take your pick. You get the idea from either one. Vlad was no Prince Charming. It is estimated that he killed between 40,000 and 100,000 people. His favorite pastime was to impale his victims upon a stake like shish kebob. His torture methods soon earned him the nickname "Vlad the Impaler." It was rumored that Vlad even drank his victims' blood.

Vlad's Crimes: Heinous or Hogwash?

Rumors of Vlad's misbehaving seem too horrible to be true, and that's because parts of his legend might be complete hogwash. We will never know the exact details because we were not there. Much of the information we get about Vlad comes from two sources: pamphlets (small books) and word of mouth. Neither of these is 100 percent reliable.

The First Victim of Tabloid Magazines

You would not be reading this book if it was not for an invention that took place during Vlad's lifetime. In 1440, the printing press was invented, and some of the first bestsellers to roll off the presses were not great works of literature but pamphlets with titles such as *The Frightening and Truly Extraordinary Story of a Wicked Blood-Drinking Tyrant Called Prince Dracula.* These pamphlets were printed by Vlad's German enemies to hurt Vlad's reputation. They were not like today's newspapers because they did not have to print the truth and were read mostly for entertainment. Today we can find something similar to Vlad's pamphlets in any grocery store checkout line—the tabloid magazine.

GET A GROUP OF TWENTY OR SO OF YOUR MOST HONEST CLASSMATES TOGETHER IN ONE LINE. HAVE THE PERSON IN THE FRONT OF THE LINE WHISPER A SECRET TO THE NEXT PERSON. THEN, HAVE THAT PERSON WHISPER THE EXACT SAME SECRET TO THE NEXT PERSON. REPEAT THIS PROCESS DOWN THE LINE. HAVE THE LAST PERSON SAY THE SECRET OUT LOUD. IS THE SECRET THE SAME AS WHEN THE FIRST PERSON TOLD IT?

Folklore Experiment

Medieval Times

PRINCE VLAD DRINKS BLOOD

FIRST GLIMPSE AT THESE SHOCKING CRIMES

THE FRIGHTENING AND TRULY EXTRAORDINARY STORY OF A WICKED, BLOOD-DRINKING TYRANT CALLED PRINCE DRACULA

Oral History and Folklore

Many tales of Vlad's blood-drinking high jinx come down through history by being told and retold. Every time a story is retold, the teller may add his or her descriptions to it. Vlad's story may have been distorted after centuries of being told again and again.

VLAD TEPES

POSTA ROMANA

Vlad the Hero

If you ask someone from Romania about Vlad, you will hear a very different story. To Romanians, Vlad was a hero who saved Romania from Ottoman invasion. They claim Vlad did what he had to do to protect his empire. Vlad was even commemorated on a Romanian postage stamp in 1976.

How to Get Rid of a Vampire?

According to legend, which of the following will kill a vampire?

1. A wooden stake through the heart.

2. A copper bullet.

3. Stones up his nose.

4. A cross in his grave.

5. A garlic pizza.

Answer: All of the above are acceptable ways to kill a vampire, but the creator of this book recommends the garlic pizza.

RICHARD III 1452–1485

Quick! Hide! I hear Uncle Richard coming . . .

OLD CROUCHBACK   KING OF ENGLAND

Richard III has the reputation for being the meanest uncle in history. In 1483, Richard's brother King Edward IV died. Edward's sons, Prince Edward V and Richard of York, were next in line for the throne. But Uncle Richard claimed Edward IV had promised to marry Lady Eleanor Butler before secretly marrying the boys' mother, Elizabeth Woodville. In the 1400s, a promise of marriage could not be broken without permission from the church. Even worse, because Edward was legally bound to his first marriage agreement, his children were not recognized as lawful or legitimate children and could not become king.

But Richard had a solution. He crowned himself king and hid the boys away in the Tower of London. The two princes soon disappeared, and no one knows what happened to them. Rumors spread that Richard had the boys killed in their sleep. Pretty dirty trick, huh? But is it true? Maybe you can solve the mystery . . .

Can you solve the mystery with help from these clues?

THE SUSPECTS

King Richard III

Richard III placed the princes in the Tower of London in 1483 and disinherited them from the throne. Rumors that the princes had been murdered started circulating that same year, but Richard never ordered an investigation to quiet the scandal.

Motive: Murdering the princes would guarantee that there were not any threats to Richard's crown.

Means: He had easy access to the princes because they were under his care.

The Duke of Buckingham

Buckingham was Richard III's friend.

Motive: Buckingham was a descendant of kings and had a strong claim to the throne. He also stood to be rewarded from Richard's rise. Some historians speculate that Richard and Buckingham had a falling out after Buckingham murdered the two princes.

Means: He too had easy access to the princes.

King Henry VII

Henry married the princes' eldest sister, Elizabeth of York. This made him fourth in line to be king.

Motive: If Henry could get rid of the two princes and Richard III, then he could become king.

Means: He had very little access to the princes but may have been able to get to them after he defeated Richard III in the battle of Bosworth Field and claimed himself to be the rightful king. But were the princes still alive at this time? Rumors had already circulated that they had been murdered.

PHYSICAL EVIDENCE

In 1930, two skeletons were found under the staircase in the Tower of London. Are these the princes' skeletons? Researchers today could run DNA tests to be positive, but that would require DNA from the boys' mother, Elizabeth Woodville. How do you get Elizabeth's DNA? You dig up her grave and cause a whole lot of ruckus! It has not been done yet, so the mystery continues . . .

TESTIMONIES

A servant of Richard III's, Sir James Tyrell, confessed to killing the princes in 1502 on Richard's orders. Tyrell made this confession after being subjected to torture by Henry VII's men. Has your brother or sister ever sat on your head until you cry "MERCY"? If not, you have a great sibling. If yes, that is sort of what confessions under torture were like.

Turn the page to find out who murdered the princes in the Tower.

Answer: YOU DECIDE

Uncle Richard had a strong motive to kill his nephews, but other people might have wished them gone too. No one really knows if the two princes were even murdered. They could have stubbed their toes and bled to death for all we know. Many historians suspect that the rumor of the boys' murder was spread by Henry VII (You'll meet Henry VII's son, Henry VIII, on page 15). Henry and Richard's family had fought for years until Henry beat the snot out of Richard's clan and crowned himself king.

Gossip Through History's Grapevine

Thomas More
He stole the crown and killed those two innocent boys. He was so evil that he was deformed, with his right shoulder higher. Or maybe it was the left?

William Shakespeare
Sweet tale from thine lad Thomas More! I shall use it to write a play about Richard, "the poisonous bunch-backed toad."

The ghost of Henry VII
Ah-ha-ha—that Shakespeare cracks me up! Old Crouchback should never have crossed my family. Keep up the good work, Will.

Thomas More was only seven years old when Richard died. Years later, More wrote a biography about Richard called *The History of King Richard III.*

William Shakespeare wrote a play called *Richard III* that portrayed Richard as an evil villain. He used More's writings as a resource.

Henry VII had a strong motive to make Richard look bad, because his family had been feuding with Richard's for years.

Richard III was a hunchback with a withered arm. True or False?

Turn the page to find out . . .

Modern Historians

He's innocent!

He's guilty!

Modern historians still can't agree. The princes' disappearance has caused so much debate that Richard even has a fan club of defenders called the Richard III Society.

The Trial of Richard III
More Than Five Hundred Years Later

In a court of law, rumors are not evidence of guilt and are called hearsay. In 1998, a mock trial was chaired by the chief justice of the United States, the Honorable William H. Rehnquist. The chief justice found that there was not enough evidence to convict Richard and stated that the accounts of More and Shakespeare were merely "rumor on rumor."

Answer: FALSE

No one who met Richard in person mentioned a withered arm or hunched back, and that's the kind of thing you might remember. It is possible that Richard had a slightly higher shoulder from carrying heavy armor. A rumor usually starts small and grows. Here is how this one grew:

During 1514–18, the historian Thomas More wrote a biography about Richard, which described him as having one arm higher than the other. But More had never even met Richard. Years later, the great playwright William Shakespeare read More's writings and took the description of Richard a step further. In his play *Richard III,* Shakespeare described Richard as having a mangled arm and a hunched back and even wrote that dogs howled when Richard came near. You have to be pretty ugly to make dogs howl!

Science Weighs In

Scientists today can sometimes determine when a painting was created by using X-ray photography. These X-rays show the different stages that the artist used in creating the paintings and often reveal hidden paintings beneath the top layer of paint. X-rays of Richard's portrait show that Richard's shoulder line was changed . . . years after it was painted.

CREEPY FACT

Want to know what queens and kings really looked like? The most accurate portraits were death masks. A death mask is a wax or plaster mold of the person's face taken at the time of his or her death. Some of the most famous death masks were made by Madame Tussaud during the French Revolution. Madame Tussaud made a wax molding of Marie Antoinette's head right after it was chopped off.

Read more about Marie Antoinette on page 49.

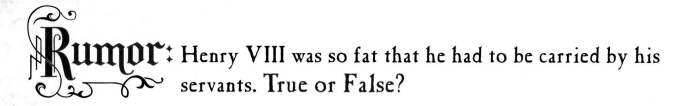

Rumor: Henry VIII was so fat that he had to be carried by his servants. True or False?

PLATE # 345

KING OF ENGLAND

HENRY VIII

1491–1547

When most people think of Henry VIII, they picture a fat old man who looks like he has a few acorns, and maybe a whole squirrel, stuffed in his mouth. But when Henry was a young man, he made all the ladies blush. Good old Hank had the Tudor supermodel body—tall and brawny.

Later in life, Henry sent the ladies running. Henry had a leg wound that oozed pus and prevented him from getting much exercise. He became so fat that his servants had to carry him in an enclosed chair supported by poles on the front and back.

Henry was a good-looking guy in his younger days.

Henry also had swollen gums, loose teeth, and horrible breath! Doctors today believe Henry's swollen face was caused by a disease called scurvy. People got scurvy when they didn't have enough vitamin C in their diet. In Henry's court, people mostly ate eels, whales, porpoises, boars, snails, peacocks, and swans. If it moved, they ate it. They didn't eat as many vitamin-rich fruits or vegetables, which might explain why Henry got so fat.

Errrrrr. Make way for the errrr . . . king!

The Tudor Taxi

Henry's weight was estimated at more than three hundred pounds. It took four servants to carry his six foot, two inch body!

HENRY'S MENU

Boar's Head
Pigeon Pie
Swan Pudding
Roasted Eel
Pickled Pig's Feet
Whole Baked Fish with Spices and Prunes
(Served only on Wednesdays, Fridays, and Sundays)

Dessert

Marzipan Cake
Quince Marmalade

Beverages

Ale, Mulled Cider, Spiced Red Wine

A Meal Fit for a King

If you are going to eat dinner at Henry's place, then you'd better bring an appetite! Henry's guests ate 4,500 to 5,000 calories (that's twice what we eat per day). A banquet meal could have as many as twenty-four courses.

To hide his expanding girth, Henry began wearing padded clothes with puffy sleeves. Out of respect for the king, everyone at court started wearing padded clothing too, and a new trend was born—fat clothes!

Spin the Ax

Using clues on the following page, can you guess which of Henry's wives got her head chopped off with an ax?

Turn to page 20 to find out . . .

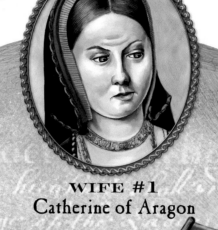

WIFE #1
Catherine of Aragon

WIFE #6
Katherine Parr

WIFE #2
Anne Boleyn

The Six Wives of Henry VIII

WIFE #5
Kathryn Howard

WIFE #3
Jane Seymour

WIFE #4
Anne of Cleves

The clues

1. Catherine of Aragon

Catherine was first married to Henry's brother, Arthur. When Arthur died, Henry married Catherine, but twenty years later he felt guilty about it.

2. Anne Boleyn

Henry dumped Catherine to marry Anne. Anne had a very thin neck.

3. Jane Seymour

Jane kept her mouth shut most of the time. She gave Henry his much-desired son, Edward VI.

4. Anne of Cleves

Anne was loud and skinny—two things Henry hated. She reminded him of a horse.

5. Kathryn Howard

Henry called Kathryn his "rose without a thorn," until he caught her in a very thorny love affair with Thomas Culpepper.

6. Katherine Parr

Katherine was really in love with Jane's brother, Thomas Seymour.

Answer: Only Kathryn Howard

1: Divorced, 2: Beheaded, 3: Died, 4: Divorced, 5: Beheaded, 6: Survived

Henry did order two of his wives to be executed, but Anne Boleyn's head was removed with a sword, not an ax.

Henry's love troubles began with his first wife, Catherine of Aragon. They were married for nearly twenty years, but never had a son survive for more than a couple of months. Henry desperately needed a son to take over the all-important job of being king. At this time, Anne Boleyn, one of Catherine's dark-eyed ladies in waiting, had caught Henry's eye. Henry fell in love with Anne and believed that she would give him a son. He had only one problem. Henry couldn't marry Anne while he was married to Catherine, so he asked the pope for an annulment to his marriage. An annulment of marriage would mean the marriage was illegal, null, void, never existed, and basically let Henry call a "do over" and get rid of Catherine. Henry might have got his divorce if the pope's home in Rome had not been sacked by Catherine's Spanish nephew, Emperor Charles V. Charles didn't want Aunt Catherine dumped so he held the pope captive and pressured him to stall on granting Henry a divorce.

But Henry was not a patient man. Instead of waiting for the pope's signature, Henry gave himself the fancy-pants title of Supreme Head of the Church of England. This puffed-up title gave Henry the power to grant *himself* a divorce. All this raucous bickering between the pope and the king led to a series of acts called the English Reformation. To reform means to change, and that is exactly what the English Reformation did. Henry shut down the pope's monasteries and separated the Church of England from the Church of Rome. He then sent Catherine away so he could marry Anne.

(Read more about Anne on page 22.)

In Henry's court, a lady in waiting was a servant to the queen who would accompany the queen wherever she went . . . sort of like a paid friend. Would you trust a paid friend?

Rumor: Anne Boleyn was really a witch with six fingers, three breasts, and moles all over her body. True or False?

ANNA · BOLINA — ANG · REGINA

ANNE BOLEYN
QUEEN OF ENGLAND, 1501/1507–1536

Answer: FALSE

Queen Anne Boleyn was not a witch, and she did not have six fingers. One of her biographers, George Wyatt, wrote that Anne had an extra fingernail. An extra fingernail could easily have been exaggerated to become an extra finger. Anne did have many enemies who were quick to spread rumors, and people just love to gossip about extra fingers.

This rumor could also have started with a priest named Nicholas Sander who wrote a biography about Anne after her death. In his biography, Sander claimed that Anne was a witch with six fingers, moles on her neck, three breasts, and a projected tooth. Now, that's a bit much! Sander never even met Anne, but people believed the rumor and still talk about Anne's six fingers today.

Anne Boleyn was so hated by the people of England that they even blamed her for a bad harvest, as if she really did have magical powers.

Anne: The Most Hated

In 1533, everyone was talking about the scandal. Henry VIII had dumped his first wife, Catherine of Aragon, and broken away from the Catholic Church in order to marry Anne Boleyn. In the sixteenth century, divorces were rare, but a king's behavior was often copied by his subjects. If the king could get rid of his wife, then what was to stop other men from doing the same? Women especially were terrified of a "get rid of your wife" trend, and they blamed Anne, not Henry.

Despite Anne's unpopularity, Henry had fallen desperately in love with her and hoped that she would give him a son. Disappointment set in when Anne gave birth to a girl, the future Queen Elizabeth I. Anne became pregnant three more times, but the babies never survived birth. People gossiped that Anne could not conceive a healthy son because she was a witch. On top of the silly court gossip, Henry became tired of Anne's grumpiness and complaining about his girlfriends. Always fickle, Henry got a new crush on one of Anne's demure ladies in waiting, Jane Seymour . . .

Then Anne's greatest enemy delivered the final blow. The Spanish emperor, Charles V, hinted that if Henry dumped Anne, Spain would form an alliance with England. Henry desperately needed Spain's support against his enemy, France. The best way to quickly get rid of Anne was to make her a head shorter.

Bewitching Love

Henry wrote passionate love letters to Anne during their courtship. Seventeen of those letters have survived. Can you guess which of the love letters below is the real letter?

A.
Methinketh my heart aches to kiss thy every mole and place a ring on one of your six fingers...
Your loving servant,

B.
...let me know expressly your whole mind as to the love between us two. It is absolutely necessary for me to obtain this answer, having been for above a whole year stricken with the dart of love...

Answer: B. Hank really was struck with the love arrow. We don't know how Anne responded to this gushing display of affection because her letters have been lost.

23

The Wicked Witch Is Dead

Only three years after Henry married Anne, she was tried and convicted of adultery and plotting to kill the king. Henry claimed that Anne had seduced him through witchcraft, but those charges were never brought forward at her trial. Anne denied any wrongdoing. None of the charges against her can be proven today, but the rumors of her witch-like appearance and powers live on.

On May 17, 1536, Anne was beheaded on Tower Green, and Henry married Jane Seymour eleven days later. In 2006, a memorial to commemorate Anne's death was built on her execution site.

A MOST
Certain, Strange, and true Difcovery of a

VVITCH.

Signs that **you** might be a witch in the sixteenth century:

1. You have a birthmark or a scar.
2. You like to eat babies.
3. You have six fingers.
4. You float when dunked under water.
5. You own a cat.
6. You fly through the night on your broomstick.

NOT JUST GOSSIP . . .

An estimated 40,000 people were killed during the witch-hunts of the fifteenth through seventeenth centuries. One of the most obvious signs of witchcraft was a deformity. You could be burned to death for a simple birthmark! And if you had six fingers, you can forget about marrying the king of England. You would be lucky to get a toad to marry you.

Answers:

3 out of 5:
You are definitely a witch. You probably get giddy when you see a broomstick and can't stop licking toads.

2 out of 5:
You could be a witch. Knock on wood three times and walk backwards for a day and you should be cured.

0 out of 5:
Congratulations! You are not a witch. You're a model citizen of the sixteenth century. You sink like a rock in water and can safely use a broomstick to clean.

Rumor: Anne of Cleves looked like a horse. True or False?

№ 2379
ANNE OF CLEVES

QUEEN OF ENGLAND
1515 – 1557

Answer: YOU DECIDE

A Portrait Can Lie

Being the court painter was not an easy gig. In many cases, the portraits had to be flattering or the artist might be punished severely. The most famous painter in Henry VIII's court was Hans Holbein. One day, Henry sent Holbein to paint portrait miniatures of two German princesses, Amelia and Anne of Cleves. A portrait miniature is a very small painting that measures about one and a half by one and a quarter inches. Henry used Holbein's paintings to decide which sister to marry. When Henry saw both portraits, he chose Anne as his wife. Unfortunately, when he met Anne in person, he said she looked more like a "Flanders mare" than Holbein's painting. Soon, everyone at court was talking about Anne and her horse face, but did she really look like a horse?

Ahh, yes. I will marry her. She is beautiful . . . I think?

Anne did have smallpox scars that were not included in Holbein's paintings. Most likely, Anne was just not Henry's type. Anne was thin and Henry said, "I am a big person and have need of a big wife."

Henry decided to marry Anne after seeing the above painting. Does Anne look like a horse to you? Do you think it would be hard to see what someone looked like in a painting the size of a meatball?

Rumor: Mary plotted to assassinate her cousin Elizabeth I. True or False?

MARY I
QUEEN OF SCOTLAND
1542–1587

ELIZABETH I
QUEEN OF ENGLAND
1533–1603

After Henry VIII had ordered the beheading of Elizabeth's mom, Anne Boleyn, Elizabeth became illegitimate. An illegitimate child was not typically allowed to become queen or wear any of the fancy jewelry. But Henry liked to make up his own rules. In his will, he restored Elizabeth to her place in line for the English throne. According to the will, Henry's grandniece, Mary of Scotland, wasn't even in line. If fact, Henry decreed that she was to never sit her pretty Scottish fanny on an English throne . . . ever! (Henry never liked the Scots.) Mary believed that she should be queen because Elizabeth was illegitimate and shouldn't be prancing around in pearls.

Would Mary stoop so low as to plot to have her cousin killed? *Turn the page to find out . . .*

Answer: UNCONFIRMED

Queen of the Sharpest Spades

Elizabeth really had it rough. At the age of three, she lost her mother and her title of princess. At age twenty-one, she was accused of treason by her half sister, Bloody Mary, and locked in the Tower of London.* By age twenty-five, she had escaped all of this drama and was crowned queen of England. Elizabeth was a survivor and she didn't intend to lose her crown to her upstart cousin.

Queen of Broken Hearts

Now imagine being a pampered princess, six feet tall, with oodles of good looks and charm and the finest education in the world. You would have a pretty good life, right? Wrong, if you are Mary Queen of Scots. While Elizabeth always kept her head in matters of the heart, Mary's love life caused a lot of raucousness.

The Soap Opera Begins . . .

At the age of sixteen, Mary became the queen of France when she married Francis II. But just a year later, Francis died of an ear infection. After his death, Mary decided to return to Scotland and remarry. She was offered a slew of marriage proposals from wannabe kings, but finding a husband in Mary's day was not an easy task. The person not only had to be royalty but also had to have the same religion and a hefty pile of cash stuffed in the royal mattress. None of the proposals made Mary's heart go pitter-patter until she met Lord Darnley. Darnley was Catholic, royal, rich, tall, handsome, and unfortunately a bumbling drunk. Mary didn't catch on to Darnley's nasty drinking habit until she had already married him. They were married for about two years until Darnley was curiously found strangled in the gardens in his pajamas . . . after the house he was staying in exploded!

Lord Darnley

Mary's second husband was Lord Darnley. He was tall, thin, and handsome, and treated Mary terribly. He was soon found strangled to death.

Earl of Bothwell

Mary's third husband, the Earl of Bothwell, was the chief suspect in Darnley's murder. People suspected that Mary was in on the plot, because she married Bothwell shortly after Darnley's murder.

*There were two Marys in Elizabeth's life—her half sister Mary (otherwise known as Bloody Mary) and her cousin Mary Queen of Scots.

Everywhere That Mary Went, the Rumors Were Sure to Follow

The chief suspect in Darnley's murder was Mary's pal, the Earl of Bothwell. Bothwell was the typical bad boy that mothers warn their daughters about—handsome, arrogant, and always getting into trouble. Mary must have missed that lesson, because she decided to make him husband number three. Everyone believed Bothwell murdered Darnley. But worst of all, Mary also looked guilty when she married the prime suspect in her husband's murder. The Scots couldn't accept Mary's new husband and they forced her to give up her crown.

Mary was then locked up in Lochleven Castle, but with help from one of her admirers, William Douglas, she escaped in the dead of night. Mary couldn't stay in Scotland because her people now hated her. Where would Mary go?

Out of the Frying Pan, into the Fire

Mary decided to flee to England against her advisors' wishes. We don't know exactly what her advisors said, but it might have been along the lines of "Say Mary, going to England is a really daffy idea." Mary's visit to England put Elizabeth in a dangerous position. Mary was Catholic. Elizabeth was Protestant. Many powerful Catholics (such as the pope) wanted Mary on the throne instead of Elizabeth, and Elizabeth was in no mood to lose her crown in a popularity contest. So she did what any sensible queen would do with an unwanted visit from a relative. She locked Mary up.

Mary spent the next nineteen years of her life confined in England. Mary's prison didn't have bars. Her prison was a house, so it was more like being grounded or sent to your room without television . . . for nineteen years.

What should I do today? Write more letters in code? Maybe embroider another unicorn tapestry?

Passing Notes Can Get You Beheaded!

Supposedly, Mary smuggled some incriminating notes out of her prison, letters that revealed plans to assassinate Elizabeth. The letters were passed to a fellow conspirator named Anthony Babington who had always had a bit of a crush on Mary (many men did). These letters were written in a secret code in which fifty-nine symbols represented letters and phrases. But Queen Elizabeth was a tad better at the whole espionage thing. She had a crack team of supersleuths that would have put modern-day Scotland Yard to shame. One of Elizabeth's spies intercepted the letters and deciphered the code. When Elizabeth read Mary's plans to assassinate her, she still refused to order Mary's execution. But Elizabeth's advisors convinced Elizabeth that Mary had to go. After much stalling, Elizabeth signed Mary's death warrant.

"You have planned in divers ways and manners to take my life and ruin my kingdom by the shedding of blood. I never proceeded so harshly against you. On the contrary I have maintained you and preserved your life with the same care which I use for myself."

Elizabeth R

Elizabeth wrote to Mary after she found out about the assassination plot. Elizabeth was obviously really ticked off. But Mary could argue that Elizabeth wasn't doing her any favors by locking her up for nineteen years.

Can You Crack the Code?

While Mary was imprisoned, Babington sent her letters using part of the secret code or cipher below. In this cipher, each symbol replaced a letter of the alphabet or a small word like "but," "there," or "my." Using Babington's cipher, can you crack the secret message below? Just substitute a letter or word for each of the coded symbols. *Answer hidden on page 60.*

a	b	c	d	e	f	g	h	i	k	l	m	n	o	p	q	r	s	t	u	x	y	z

that	if	but	where	as	of	the	so	there	this	in	I	pray	you	me	my

(cipher symbols shown above each entry)

(Coded message in cipher symbols)

Hint: The Elizabethan alphabet had only twenty-four letters instead of the standard twenty-six. The letters *u* and *v* were the same letter and the letters *i* and *j* were also the same. Elizabethans also often used two *v*'s instead of a letter *w*. In the above example, use the letter *i* to replace *j*. Use the letter *u* instead of *v*. You won't need the *w*.

? **Where are the j, v, and w?**

Parts of Babington's Letter to Mary
(Translated from Code)

"Myself with ten gentlemen and a hundred of our followers will undertake the delivery of your royal person from the hands of your enemies.

For the dispatch of the usurper, from the obedience of whom we are by the excommunication of her made free, there be six noble gentlemen, all my private friends, who for the zeal they bear to the Catholic cause and your Majesty's service will undertake that tragical execution...

I will be at Lichfield, expecting your Majesty's answer and letters, in readiness to execute what by them shall be commanded."

Your Majesty's most faithful subject and sworn servant,"

Anthonie Babington

Elizabeth is the "usurper," because Babington believed that Mary was the rightful queen of England.

Translation: Do away with Elizabeth!

Babington did not want to commit to killing Elizabeth without Mary's approval.

Was Mary Guilty?

In his letter, Babington asked Mary to sanction Elizabeth's execution. The letter was intercepted by Elizabeth's spies, who cracked the code, sealed it back up, and sent it along to Mary to wait for her response. Supposedly, Mary's response was to go forward with the plot. Mary now looked very guilty! But wait a minute. Have you seen Mary's original letter? No? Neither has anyone. The original letter disappeared and only copies remain today. At her trial, Mary claimed her response to Babington's letter was a forgery. But her word did not matter.

Mary was convicted of treason and was beheaded at Fotheringhay Castle on February 8, 1587.

Elizabeth's Side

As long as Mary was alive, Catholic conspirators would try to put Mary on Elizabeth's throne. Elizabeth knew that a Catholic queen in a Protestant land would stir up religious wars. She also feared that Spain or France would declare war against England if she executed Mary. What she really wanted was for a tree to fall on Mary, or some other unfortunate accident. Certainly if Mary was assassinated . . . Elizabeth knew *she* could not be held responsible. Always a master of plots, Elizabeth signed Mary's death warrant, but told her secretary not to deliver it. If the execution was carried out without her written consent, then she could not be held responsible. Right? But Elizabeth's naughty council disobeyed Elizabeth and delivered the death warrant. When she heard the execution had been carried out, Elizabeth appeared deeply upset and demanded to know who had ordered such a thing!

Did Elizabeth order the death of an innocent queen?

Dear Mary, God's teeth! I can't believe you would try to kill me!

Elizabeth and Mary wrote to each other many times, but never met face-to-face. Their opinions of each other were based mainly on gossip from others.

Mary's Side

Babington confessed that Mary had plotted to kill Elizabeth, but his confession was most likely obtained through torture. At her trial, Mary demanded to see the original letters from her to Babington, but the court could produce only copies of the letters. Mary argued that the letters were forgeries because they lacked her signature. She admitted her desire to escape her prison but denied any intent to harm Elizabeth. It is possible that Mary knew nothing of the plots to assassinate Elizabeth. It is also possible that Mary wouldn't have thought twice about ripping Elizabeth's crown off her wigged head. Without all the facts, we can only gossip about this misguided queen.

Did Mary deserve her fate?

Dear Elizabeth,
Don't believe the rumors. Your council is trying to frame me!

Mary knew that her execution would shock the rest of the world. At her trial she said, "Remember that the theatre of the world is wider than the realm of England."

Queen Elizabeth's Favorite Things

Do you know which are true?

1. Mice

2. Succory porridge

3. Ale

4. The Spanish

5. Shakespeare

6. Dancing

7. Cursing

8. Pirates

9. Chopping heads off

10. The dentist

11. Bear-baiting

Answer:

1. **No.** Elizabeth was brave when her half sister, Mary I (Bloody Mary), imprisoned her in the Tower of London. She laughed at the Spanish invading her borders. She stood up to her council when they pestered her to marry. But show her a beady-eyed, disease-spreading rodent and she'd scream like a schoolgirl.

2. **Yes.** Succory porridge is like eating dandelions in your oatmeal. Yummy.

3. **Yes.** She drank ale in the morning with her porridge because it was not safe to drink water.

Gross Fact

In the 1500s, being a mouse was not half bad. Cats had become unpopular because they were believed to be witches *(see page 21)*. No cats around, nobody to kill the mice. Mice could raucously run around the palace, scaring the queen and eating her porridge. They just had to be careful of the mice killing dogs. That's right. Dogs were taught to kill mice!

4. **No.** England wasn't getting along with Spain. The Spanish were a little sore after England sank their greatest fleet of ships, the Spanish Armada.

5. **Yes. (Sort of.)** Imagine that you live in Elizabethan times and have nothing to do. You could either watch a public execution, bear-baiting, or a play. Wouldn't you pick the play? Elizabeth especially loved Shakespeare's comedies, and he even put on private readings for Elizabeth and her court. It was rumored that Elizabeth's favorite play was *The Merry Wives of Windsor* . . . a comedy full of trickery! But Elizabeth died at the rise of Shakespeare's popularity. Shakespeare's greatest works were performed during the reign of Elizabeth's sucessor, James VI.

Playwright & Pot Stirrer

Although Shakespeare had a great passion for history, his plays were meant to be only dramatic, not factual. In fact, Shakespeare was the ultimate rumor spreader. He actually invented the word *gossip*, along with several other English words. He wrote plays about English kings that many people wrongly believed were based on true events. One of his plays especially hurt the reputation of Richard III. *See page 10 to read more.*

6. **Yes.** She especially enjoyed a dance called the Volta, which involved jumping high into the air. You might have thought all this jumping up and down looked silly, but it was the thing to do then.

7. **Yes.** Elizabeth could be majestic and regal one minute and then swear like a street merchant the next. She didn't use any of the curse words that we know today. If she stubbed her toe you might catch her saying, "God's teeth . . . peevish lily-livered ratsbane!!"

8. **Yes.** At the start of Elizabeth's reign, England was deep in debt. At the end of her reign, the national debts had been cleared. How did Elizabeth do it? She had a little help from her personal pirate, Sir Francis Drake. With Elizabeth's blessing, Drake plundered booty in gold, silver, and spices from Spanish ships. Elizabeth even rewarded Drake for his thievery by knighting him.

9. **No.** She hated to sign death warrants, and when it was required, she usually had the offender burned or hung. Beheading was reserved for the lucky nobility. Elizabeth's dad, Henry VIII, ordered more executions than any other English monarch in history.

10. **No.** Elizabeth was terrified of the dentist. She once made her dentist pull out her archbishop's tooth so she could see if it hurt *before* her dentist pulled her tooth. Elizabeth liked her sweets, which eventually caused her teeth to turn black and fall out. In the sixteenth century, it was a sign of wealth to have black teeth because most people could not afford sweets. People even painted their teeth black to look like they had tooth decay!

11. **Yes.** Parents think today's video games are violent, but they should have seen what the Elizabethan kids did for fun. Bear-baiting was watching a helpless bear being torn to shreds by a pack of dogs.

How to Flatter Like an Elizabethan

Want to get an A on that book report? Try giving this compliment to your teacher:

"Thou art a flowering young-eyed, wafer-cake!"

Disclaimer: Results not guaranteed.

How to Curse Like an Elizabethan

Next time your parents ask you to go to bed, try this one out:

"Jarring rump-fed apple-john, I shall not go to thou saucy motley-minded hedge-pig bed!"

Disclaimer: Do not try this if your parents are Elizabethan historians.

Royal Crushes: Secret Pages from Elizabeth's Diary

Elizabeth is known as the Virgin Queen because she chose not to marry. But don't think she never got any offers. She was beautiful. She was witty. She could flirt in eight languages (Greek, French, Italian, Latin, Spanish, Flemish, Welsh, and, of course, English). This sassy, vibrant redhead was a real heartbreaker.

Stuffy old Philip wearing black . . . again.

Dear Diary,
I can't believe that grumpy-pants king of Spain asked me to marry him! As if I would marry someone who only dresses in black and spends all his time chasing Protestants out of Spain. Nobody in England wants a Spanish king. And how weird would it be to marry your dead sister's husband? God's teeth!

Philip II

One of Elizabeth's first marriage proposals came from the king of Spain, Philip II. Philip had been married to Elizabeth's older half sister, Bloody Mary. Mary had ordered thousands of Protestants burnt to a crisp. After Mary's death, Elizabeth was crowned queen and everyone breathed a sigh of relief. Everyone except Philip. Philip thought he should remain king of England, so he proposed to Elizabeth. Elizabeth said no thanks and told Philip that is was just too weird to marry your dead sister's husband. True, it would have been weird, but that was not the real reason. After Mary's craziness, Elizabeth and the rest of her kingdom didn't want a Spanish Catholic ruler in England.

"I would rather be a beggar and single than a queen and married."
—Elizabeth to the ambassador of the Duke of Wurtemberg, 1564.

Sweet bottom grass, I'll bathe my lips in rosy dews of kisses.

Eric XIV

Eric XIV always thought people were laughing at him behind his back. They probably were. He wooed Elizabeth by writing her love letters in Latin and challenging her master of the horse, Robert Dudley, to duels. After many years of not giving an answer (Elizabeth always kept her suitors waiting), Elizabeth declined his marriage proposal.

Robert Dudley

Robert Dudley, nicknamed "Robin," was Elizabeth's greatest love. Not only could he match Elizabeth's sharp wit, but he also was a royal catch—tall, dark, and handsome. He could charm the flies off Elizabeth's horse. But Elizabeth could not choose a husband based on how he looked in tights. She had to choose a husband of royal birth. Her group of advisors, called her Privy Council, also had to approve her marriage. Her council did not approve of her marrying Dudley because he was not a prince or a duke . . . and he also had the little problem of already being married!

Elizabeth and Dudley continued to flirt, and rumors of their relationship spread throughout the court. People even gossiped that they had already married. In one rumor, Elizabeth had been pregnant with Dudley's child. None of these rumors was true. Then, to add fuel to the fire, Dudley's wife took a tumble down the stairs, broke her neck, and died. Dudley's enemies whispered that he had killed his wife so that he could marry Elizabeth. Dudley was eventually cleared of the charges, but the damage was done. Rumors now threatened Elizabeth's popularity. In the end, Elizabeth decided she couldn't marry Dudley, but they remained friends throughout their lives.

Elizabeth + Robert XO XO True Love 4-ever My Dear Robin

Duke of Anjou

Elizabeth lovingly called Francois, Duke of Anjou, her "frog." Elizabeth first said no to his proposal. Then she said maybe. Then she said yes. Then she said no again. Elizabeth always had a hard time making up her mind, but this decision was especially tough. She couldn't marry a French Catholic without causing a serious ruckus. Sadly, she had to send her little amphibian hopping back to France.

Why did Queen Elizabeth never marry?

1. She was afraid that by choosing one suitor, the others would get angry.
2. She liked having all the power of a queen and didn't want to share it with a husband.
3. All the suitable bachelors were Catholic. Elizabeth feared that marrying a Catholic would make her unpopular with her Protestant subjects.
4. She didn't really like boys.

No one really knows why Elizabeth chose not to marry, but 1, 2 and, 3 of the answers above could have been correct. Answer 4 is not true. Elizabeth loved to be surrounded by handsome suitors and did come close to marrying.

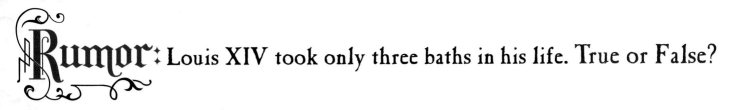

Rumor: Louis XIV took only three baths in his life. True or False?

BATH TIME FOR LOUIS

PLATE # 7325   LOUIS XIV, KING OF FRANCE   *1638–1715*

Answer: FALSE

In Louis's day, people thought a good, thick, grimy layer of filth would keep you healthy and strong! They believed water spread diseases by penetrating the pores of the skin and then infecting the bloodstream. Most people didn't bathe more than once a year. Ironically, Louis was so clean that he was almost fussy about it. He often bathed in a big Turkish bath in his palace at Versailles. When not in his bath, he rubbed spirits or alcohol on his skin, which acted as a disinfectant.

A Typical Spa Day in the Seventeenth Century

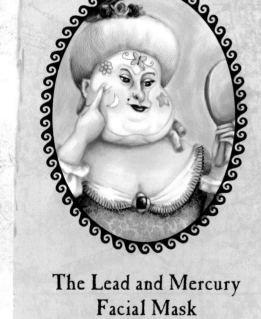

The Lead and Mercury Facial Mask

In Louis's day, both women and men wore a heavy white makeup consisting of mercury, lead, egg whites, and vinegar. Unfortunately, this beauty concoction was poisonous and caused ugly scars and blemishes. To hide the scars, it became fashionable for men and women to wear patches cut into shapes of stars, moons, and diamonds.

The Blood-Sucking Body Wrap

When Louis was sick, he was treated to a blood-sucking treatment called bloodletting. Sluglike worms called leeches were applied to the skin and allowed to suck out the blood. It was believed that these leeches cleansed the blood and rid the body of diseases. Leeches do thin the blood, allowing it to flow better, but doctors in Louis's day got a little carried away and sometimes bled their patients to death.

The Puppy Love Purifier

To improve their complexions, wealthy men and women would rub the urine from a puppy on their face. Queen Elizabeth even used urine on her teeth to whiten them. Yummy!

And, as if that were not enough, he changed his undies three times a day! All of this cleanliness must have paid off, because Louis lived to the ripe old age of seventy-seven and was king for seventy-two years, longer than any other French monarch in history.

The Squirrel Cheeks Wax Lift

Women would often stick wax balls in their cheeks, called "plumpers" to fill them out. In Louis's day, a rounded face was considered far more beautiful than a thin one. In fact, the more meat you had on your bones, the better!

The Boil Butt Beautifier

In the seventeenth century, men would often get painful ulcers on their rear ends from the constant horseback riding. Louis XIV got such a bad boil on his butt that he had to have it lanced by his doctor. In an effort to copy the king, Louis's subjects begged their doctors to cut their bottoms . . . even if they lacked the boil.

Le Petite King

Louis XIV towered over his subjects at an amazing six feet, ten inches. Unfortunately, he was only five feet, four inches when naked. To compensate for his short stature, he wore a twelve-inch-high wig and six-inch red heels. But this was one look that no one could copy. Louis decreed that only the king could wear red heels.

Peter Was a Monster

By Dr. Noah Itallsky

President, Peter Was a Big Jerk Society

Peter was a loudmouthed, drunken bully. When he got sick of his bossy half sister telling him what to do, he locked her in a convent. Later, he locked his first wife, poor dear Eudoxia, in a convent too, because she was too Russian for him. He even had his son tortured to death. Peter's second wife was named Sophia, but that sounded too outdated, so he gave her the more modern name of Catherine. Catherine could bend iron bars with her bare hands and drink as much vodka as Peter. She wasn't any Russian wallflower.

PETER I
CZAR OF RUSSIA
1672–1725

Peter forced the people of Russia to build a new capital just so he could be nearer to the sea and build his ships. Then he had the nerve to name the city after himself. Thousands died building the city of St. Petersburg with their bare hands. They called St. Petersburg the city "built on bones."

Peter died in 1725. Thank goodness he died before he could hurt Russia further.

Raucous Royals Disclaimer: The above historians are not available for comment because they do not exist.

Which historian is right?

Peter Was a Saint

By Professor Sara Rosey
President, Peter the Great Fan Club

PETER I
CZAR OF RUSSIA
1672–1725

Peter was an energetic, decisive leader. Peter's half sister ruled in Peter's place until he was old enough to rule himself. Then, she retired to a convent. Peter's first wife, Eudoxia, retired to a convent also because she wanted to be closer to God. Peter had one son but he tried to steal Peter's throne, so Peter was forced to have him executed. Peter's second wife was named Sophia, but Peter adoringly called her Catherine. She was a cheerful lady who matched Peter's energy. She was his treasured Russian rose.

Peter moved Russia's capital from the landlocked Moscow to a coastal location so he could build the first Russian navy. He named the city after his patron saint, Saint Peter. Thousands admired the new city along the water. They called St. Petersburg the "window on Europe."

Peter died in 1725. Too bad he died before he could finish all his plans.

To many critics, Peter was a brutal tyrant who forced his policies on Russia at the price of precious lives. Thousands of Russians fled to other countries to escape Peter's forced labor and the army draft. When a male of a Russian family was drafted into Peter's army, the family would have a funeral because they knew they would never see their son again. And while Peter was out behaving like a naughty frat boy, his people struggled to put food on the table.

His supporters would point out that everything Peter did was for the good of Russia. Peter saw change as necessary for his country's survival. With the energy of ten men, he built up the first Russian navy, reorganized the army, opened schools, and expanded Russia's territories. And he accomplished all of this while consuming large amounts of vodka and partying like a rock star. When Peter died, he left behind a Russia with a powerful army and a new modern capital where art and new ideas could flourish.

Whether you think Peter is a big jerk or a dynamic leader, he is undoubtedly a fascinating character in the history of Russia.

Peter the Dentist

You would never want to complain about a toothache around Peter. Dr. Pete was great at ripping out teeth, but he didn't really care if it hurt or not.

Peter the Barber

Peter hated beards so much that he would rip a beard out by the roots if he caught anyone wearing one. He thought mustaches were much more civilized.

Rumor:
When told the poor did not have bread, Marie Antoinette said, "Let them eat cake." True or False?

PLATE # 765

MARIE ANTOINETTE, QUEEN OF FRANCE
MADAME DEFICIT   1755-1793

Answer:

Marie never uttered the famous line "Let them eat cake." In 1766, the philosopher Jean Jacques Rousseau claimed a "great princess" had heartlessly suggested that the poor eat cake if they had no bread. Rousseau could not have been referring to Marie, because in 1766 Marie was only eleven years old and was living in Austria. So who did say it? We may never know, but we do have a good idea why this rumor started.

Spend Now . . . Pay Later

Politics in France were unfair before Marie ever stepped her jewel-clad slipper into the country. The poor were taxed heavily while the rich didn't pay any taxes. This tax system caused the peasants and working classes to get poorer and poorer. Then, France had some nasty weather that caused a bread shortage. Marie had already developed a reputation in her teen queen days for being a shopaholic bubblehead, so everyone blamed the bread shortage on Marie, on her husband, King Louis XVI, and on the whole unfair government.

The Fishwives

Marie was nicknamed Madame Deficit and at one point had an angry crowd of fishwives try to rip her to shreds. You didn't want to mess with the fishwives. They screamed loudly, smelled like eel, and were strong enough to hack up fish.

Why All the Fuss over Bread?

Bread was the main staple of the French diet. The average French person ate two pounds of bread a day! Without bread, the poor were forced to eat street rats (which didn't taste like chicken). Wouldn't you get a bit grumpy if you had to eat rat stew every night for dinner?

Rat Stew AGAIN!!!

During France's food shortage, Marie cut back on her expenses, removed the gambling tables from her drawing room, wore simpler clothes, and took an interest in politics. Marie grew up. Unfortunately, it was too late. The rumors had already hurt her reputation, and you must know by now how hard it is to kill a rumor.

Marie's husband, Louis XIV, was sent to the guillotine on January 21, 1793. Marie soon followed on October 16, 1793. Marie Antoinette was the last queen of France.

PLATE # 1093

NAPOLEON BONAPARTE, FRENCH EMPEROR
NAPOLEON SITTING TALL

1769-1821

Napoleon was no linebacker, but he certainly was not short either. Using the old French measurement system, he was five feet, two inches, which equals five feet, six inches by modern measurements. Today, Napoleon might get picked last in basketball, but the average height in northern Europe in the late eighteenth century was five feet, four and a half inches. Napoleon was one and a half inches taller than the average man of his time!

Little Boney

Napoleon was one of the most respected generals throughout history. After trampling Austria, Russia, and Egypt, he was feared throughout Europe. But when Napoleon threatened England, the British did what any country would do with a bully trying to push them around. They came back with their own threats in the form of "Oh, yeah? Just try to get across these waters," and then followed it with some short jokes. Not just any old short jokes, but some sidesplitting cartoons of Napoleon. I guess you had to be there, but the Brits found it hilarious. The British press printed these cartoons over and over again, and eventually the short rumor stuck.

Average Adult Male Heights in Northern Europe

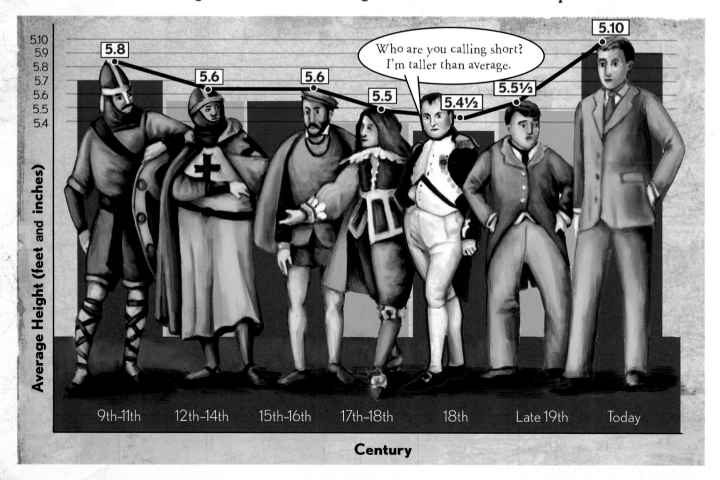

The British cartoonist James Gillray called Napoleon "Little Boney." Gillray drew Napoleon as a hot-tempered midget who threw fits when he didn't get his way. In this cartoon to the left, the midget Napoleon was shown throwing globes around in a crying fit.

Hurry up and finish the painting. These stomach cramps are killing me!

True or False?

The Europeans in the seventeenth and eighteenth centuries were shorter than people today because they didn't have enough food to eat.

Napoleon always posed with his hand tucked into his waistcoat because

A. he suffered from a stomach ulcer.

B. he had a deformed hand.

C. the pose was considered polite.

D. artists hated painting hands.

ANSWERS:

TRUE. Poverty and disease were more widespread during Napoleon's time than in other centuries. Many scientists believe that people were shorter in the eighteenth and early nineteenth centuries because the peasant majority didn't have enough food to eat. Without enough food for everyone, people shrank.

C. Napoleon did suffer from stomach cramps, but he didn't strike his infamous hand-in-coat pose for any medical reason. Napoleon's pose had become popular before he was even born. Gentlemen put their hand in their waistcoat because it was considered polite, similar to how we stand up straight and smile in pictures today.

THE PET TATTLER

HEADLINES IN HISTORY...RIPPED STRAIGHT FROM THE HORSE'S MOUTH

(1)
NAPOLEON UNLUCKY ON HIS WEDDING NIGHT

MARCH 11, 1810

Napoleon Bonaparte is used to being top dog. But on his wedding night, Josephine's pug, Fortune, really showed the emperor who was boss in the boudoir. Sources say that when Napoleon climbed into bed, Fortune bit him on the calf! Josephine insisted that the dog stay Napoleon lost this battle

Read more abou Napoleon on page 5

(2)
MARY QUEEN OF SCOTS IS EXECUTED.
DOG MOURNS HER DEATH *FEBRUARY 8, 1587*

At the order of her cousin Elizabeth I, Mary Queen of Scots was beheaded at Fotheringhay Castle. Unfortunately, it took three swings of the ax to chop off her head. After the deed was done, Mary's dog popped out from underneath her red petticoat and cried by his mistress's head. He was one sad pooch.

Reports say that Philip II of Spain was none too happy about the execution and is now planning to attack England with a mean-looking fleet of ships called the Armada.

When asked about the execution, Elizabeth replied, "What execution? I didn't order any execution!"

Read more about Elizabeth and Mary on page 34.

CATHERINE THE GREAT, EMPRESS OF RUSSIA, DIED AFTER BEING CRUSHED BY HER HORSE. NOVEMBER 5, 1796,

Turn the page to find out which story is false . . .

Answer: #3 is FALSE

Catherine the Great did love horseback riding, but that is not what did her in. She died of a stroke in her bed at the ripe old age of sixty-seven. Everyone knows that it is not polite to start rumors about your empress. So who started this poppycock about Catherine's death?

THE RUMOR SUSPECTS

1. A member of the Russian Court?

The dainty ladies and dapper gentlemen of Catherine's court were shocked by her riding habits. Catherine often rode astride a horse instead of using the conventional sidesaddle. There must have been much whispering behind her back.

2. A supporter of Peter the III?

Many of Catherine's court were angry about a German empress on the throne. Catherine came to Russia from Germany to marry Peter III. Being German born, she was forbidden to rule over Russia by herself. This minor detail didn't stop her from kicking her nincompoop husband off the throne and taking his place.

3. A French enemy?

At the time of Catherine's reign, the French were going through an especially raucous period called the French Revolution. The people of France were tired of kings, queens, and useless authority figures and were having a grand old time chopping off their heads. Catherine was hopping mad about the beheading and was not a fan of torture. She spoke out against France's unruly behavior and made many French enemies.

ANSWER: 3. Most historians credit this rumor to the French upper class, because they had the means to travel and therefore spread rumors across the seas.

PLATE # 657   GEORGE III, KING OF ENGLAND
FARMER GEORGE   1738-1820

Answer: TRUE

George had periods of madness throughout his life. Being the king is definitely a high-stress job, but ruling during the American Revolution couldn't have been easy. England had massive debts due to the French and Indian War. To pay these debts, England placed a tax on the tea shipped to the American colonies. America responded to the tax by dumping George's tea in the water (George really liked his tea). George wasn't getting any respect. Americans even melted his statue. And just when things couldn't possibly get more wretched, George's doctors fed him poison! The debts, the tea, the statue, the poison . . . it was all a bit much. Can you blame George for getting wacky?

King George III talked to an oak tree because . . .

A. it talked to him first.
B. he was a good farmer and loved trees.
C. he thought it was the King of Prussia.

American revolutionaries melted down the statue of King George III to make . . .

A. cups to give George's troops some tea.
B. bullets to fire at King George's troops.
C. new teeth for George Washington.

G GEORGE III

ANSWERS: 1. C. One day, while driving through Windsor Park, George screamed, "Stop!" and got out of his coach to greet the king of Prussia. He shook hands with the man and began a polite conversation. Unfortunately, he was really talking to an oak tree.

2. B. In 1776, American revolutionaries melted the statue of poor George to make bullets.

Think going to the doctor is bad? Here was George's treatment.

Step 1:
Place burning hot cups on the king's back.

In George's day doctors believed that placing burning hot glass cups on the skin would burn out the madness. This process was called "blistering" because the burning left painful blisters on the skin.

Step 2:
Tie the king to a chair and stuff a gag in his mouth.

After getting burnt too many times, George had a habit of thrashing about and shouting out bad words. His doctors believed that tying him up would control his temper.

Step 3:
Feed him arsenic.

Doctors fed George a medicine called James Powder throughout his illness. James Powder was used to cure fevers and contained arsenic. At the time, doctors didn't understand that arsenic was poisonous. If there is one thing you don't want to feed a crazy person, it's poison. Doctors today believe that George suffered from a rare blood disorder called porphyria, which was worsened by his medicine and eventually caused poor George to go nutty.

How You Can Research a Rumor

1. Ask one question. Pick a subject that is neither too specific nor too broad. For example, more books have been written about Napoleon than any ruler in history. There is so much information written about him that it can be overwhelming. One fascinating rumor to research could be Napoleon's death. Many historians believe that Napoleon was poisoned by his enemies, but most doctors believe that he simply died of stomach cancer. Start with a small topic that most interests you. You can always expand it later.

2. Know the time period. After you have decided on what rumor to research, the next step is to dig deeper. What did the gossipers eat? What did they wear? What language did they speak? Were they

rich or poor? Look at a map to see where they lived. What was the religion and politics of that time period? Knowing the time period will give you clues to prove or disprove the rumor. For example, many historians still claim that Anne Boleyn really did have six fingers simply because of what she wore. In the 1500s, Anne started a fashion for wearing long sleeves, and many claim that she wore this style to cover up her sixth finger.

3. Get at least three versions of the story.

Everyone has a different view of history. Check at least three different sources before believing any rumor. Use encyclopedias, reference books, magazines, newspapers or microfilm, and video documentaries. Don't use only the Web. Try to use at least one current reference, because historians are discovering new facts about the past every day. For example, a recent reexamination of Napoleon's death in 2007 claimed that the emperor did die of stomach cancer. The subject is still hotly debated, but the study sheds more light on the clues surrounding his death.

It's a little-known fact that Napoleon always posed with his hand in his waistcoat because he was missing two fingers.

4. Read their mail.

You can tell a lot about someone by snooping in his or her mailbox. Mary Queen of Scots wrote over three thousand letters in her life! Visit the National Archives, the British Library, or the Library of Congress to read the original letters. Many of these letters can be accessed online, and books also print a collection of letters written by royalty. Best of all, most libraries have interlibrary loan systems, which allow members to get books from a distant library shipped to their local library.

5. Ask for help.

Don't be afraid to ask your local librarian, teacher, or parent for help. But after you get pointed in the right direction, do your own research instead of relying on the viewpoints of others. Your job is to examine all sides and come to your own conclusion. Be a history detective . . . not a rumor spreader.

ILLUSTRATION CREDITS:

Shakespeare: Folger Shakespeare Library, Washington, D.C.
Anne of Cleves, by Hans Holbein the Younger. Victoria and Albert Museum, London.
Little Boney in a strong fit, by James Gillray. National Portrait Gallery, London.
Henry at approx. age 40, by Joos van Cleeve. The Royal Collection, London.

RESOURCE NOTES:

"I am a big person and have need of a big wife": Alison Weir, *The Six Wives of Henry VIII* (New York: Grove Press, 2000), p. 382.

"Remember that the theatre of the world is wider than the realm of England": Antonia Fraser, *Mary Queen of Scots* (London: Phoenix Press, 1969), p. 507.

Love letter from Henry to Anne: Henry VIII, *Love Letters of Henry VIII to Anne Boleyn* (Boston: J. W. Luce & Company, 1906), pp. 1–2.

"You have planned in divers ways and manners to take my life and ruin my kingdom by the shedding of blood. I never proceeded so harshly against you. On the contrary I have maintained you and preserved your life with the same care which I use for myself." Jane Dunn, *Elizabeth and Mary: Cousins, Rivals, Queens* (New York: Random House, 2004), p. 395.

Babington's letter to Mary: University of Pennsylvania, referenced online at http://ccat.sas.upenn.edu/~jmcgill/abletter.html.

"rumor on rumor": Chief Justice of the United States, the Honorable William H. Rehnquist, Indiana University School of Law; referenced online at www.r3.org/trial/index.html.

The talk bubbles used throughout this book are based on research, but are not direct quotes.

BIBLIOGRAPHY

OVERALL

Cuppy, Will. *The Decline and Fall of Practically Everybody*. New York: Barnes & Noble, 1992.

Farquhar, Michael. *A Treasury of Royal Scandals*. New York: Penguin Books, 2001.

Fraser, Antonia. *The Lives of the Kings and Queens of England*. Los Angeles: University of California Press, 1999.

Lewis, Brenda Ralph. *Kings and Queens of England: A Dark History: 1066 to Present*. New York: Barnes & Noble, 2005.

Shaw, Karl. *Royal Babylon: The Alarming History of European Royalty*. New York: Broadway Books, 2001.

Shenkman, Richard. *Legends, Lies, and Cherished Myths of World History*. New York: HarperPerennial, 1994.

Tibballs, Geoff. *Royalty's Strangest Characters: Extraordinary but True Tales from 2000 Years of Mad Monarchs and Raving Rulers*. London: Robson Books, 2005.

Twiss, Miranda. *The Most Evil Men and Women in History*. New York: Barnes & Noble, 2002.

TUDOR PERIOD

Alchin, L. K. "Elizabethan Era," www.elizabethan-era.org.uk (accessed November 22, 2006).

Eakins, Lara. "Tudor History," www.tudorhistory.org (accessed November 1, 2006).

Hanson, Marilee. "Tudor England: 1485 to 1603," englishhistory.net/tudor.html (accessed November 12, 2006).

National Archives. "The Tudors," www.tudorbritain.org (accessed November 24, 2006).

Norris, Herbert. Tudor Costume and Fashion. Mineola, N.Y.: Dover Publications, 1997.

PORTRAITS

National Portrait Gallery, London.

Smith, Charles Saumarez. *The National Portrait Gallery*. London: National Portrait Gallery Publications, 2004.

Tudor and Elizabeth Portraits. www.tudor-portraits.com (accessed January 15, 2007).

CATHERINE THE GREAT

Catherine the Great. DVD. PBS, 2006.

De Madariaga, Isabel. "Catherine the Great: A Personal View." *History Today* 51, no. 11 (November 2001): 45–51.

Henderson, Simon. "Catherine the Great: Enlightened Empress?" *History Review*, no. 51 (March 2005): 14–19.

Troyat, Henri. *Catherine the Great*. New York: Dutton, 1980.

ELIZABETH I

Chamberlin, Frederick. *The Sayings of Queen Elizabeth*. London: John Lane; New York: Dodd, Mead and Company, 1923.

Culbertson, Katherine E. "Elizabeth I: The Most Elusive Bride in History," Hanover Historical Review; online at http://history hanover.edu/hhr/94/hhr94_2.html (accessed November 10, 2006).

Dunn, Jane. *Elizabeth and Mary: Cousins, Rivals, Queens*. New York: Random House, 2004.

Eakins, Lara. TudorCast podcast (accessed November 1, 2006).

Elizabeth I: The Virgin Queen. DVD. Biography, 2004.

Elizabeth's Pirates. Channel Four Television Corporation, London; www.channel4.com/history/microsites/H/history/pirates/index.html (accessed November 1, 2006).

Folger Shakespeare Library website, www.folger.edu (accessed November 20, 2006).

In Search of Shakespeare. DVD. PBS, 2004.

Jenkins, Elizabeth. *Elizabeth the Great*. New York: Coward-McCann, 1958.

Marcus, Leah S., Janel Mueller, and Beth Rose. *Elizabeth I Collected Works*. Chicago: University of Chicago Press, 2000.

MacDonogh, Katharine. *Reigning Cats and Dogs*. New York: St. Martin's Press, 1999.

Thomas, Heather. "Elizabeth R." www.elizabethi.org (accessed November 29, 2006).

GEORGE III

Bloy, Marjie. "The Age of George III." *A Web of English History*, www.historyhome.co.uk/c-eight/18chome.htm (accessed January 14, 2007).

Macalpine, Ida. *George III and the Mad-Business*. New York: Pantheon Books, 1970.

Schirber, Michael. "Doctors Poisoned Crazy King George, Study Finds." *Live Science*, www.LiveScience.com (accessed January 24, 2007).

HENRY VIII & ANNE BOLEYN

Farley, Stacey. "King Henry VIII and His Wives." *The World of Royalty*, www.royalty.nu/Europe/England/Tudor/HenryVIII.html (accessed December 1, 2006).

Henry VIII. *Love Letters of Henry VIII to Anne Boleyn*. Boston: J. W. Luce and Company, 1906.

Thurston, Robert W. "The World, the Flesh and the Devil." *History Today*, November 2006, pp. 51–57.

Warnicke, Retha M. *The Rise and Fall of Anne Boleyn*. New York: Cambridge University Press, 1989; reprint edition, 1991.

Weir, Alison. *The Six Wives of Henry VIII*. New York: Grove Press, 2000.

The Wives of Henry VIII. DVD. Channel Four Television Corporation, 2001.

HENRY VIII

Fletcher, David. *Henry VIII*. Hove, U.K.: Wayland Publishers, 1976.

Great Kings of England: King Henry VIII. DVD. Kultur Video, 2006.

Maclean Kybett, Susan. "Henry VIII—A Malnourished King?" *History Today* 39, no. 9 (September 1989): 19–25.

Weir, Alison. *Henry VIII and His Court*. New York: Ballantine Books, 2002.

LOUIS XIV

"Beauty in the Seventeenth Century." National Maritime Museum, London, www.nmm.ac.uk/server/show/nav.00500b (accessed January 15, 2007).

Fraser, Antonia. *Love and Louis XIV: The Women in the Life of the Sun King*. New York: Nan A. Talese, 2006.

Lewis, W. H. *The Splendid Century: Life in the France of Louis*. Long Grove, Ill.: Waveland Press, 1997.

Mitford, Nancy. *The Sun King*. New York: Harper & Row, 1966.

Wilkinson, Richard. "The Man in the Golden Mask." *History Review*, no. 56 (December 2006): 45–46.

MARIE ANTOINETTE

Covington, Richard. "From Beloved to Beheaded: The Real Marie Antoinette." *Smithsonian*, November 2006, pp. 56–65.

The French Revolution. DVD. History Channel, 2005.

Lever, Evelyne. *Marie Antoinette: The Last Queen of France*. New York: Farrar, Straus and Giroux, 2000.

Marie Antoinette. DVD. PBS, David Grubin Productions, 2006.

MARY QUEEN OF SCOTS

Bold, Alan Norman. *Mary, Queen of Scots*. Hove, U.K.: Wayland Publishers, 1977.

Fraser, Antonia. *Mary Queen of Scots*. London: Phoenix Press, 1969.

Harlot or Martyr? The Case of Mary Stuart. VHS. Films for the Humanities & Sciences, 1999.

Mumby, Frank Arthur. *The Fall of Mary Stuart: A Narrative in Contemporary Letters*. Boston: Houghton Mifflin Company, 1922.

Singh, Simon. *The Code Book: The Evolution of Secrecy from Mary Queen of Scots to Quantum Cryptography*.
New York: Doubleday, 1999.

Sitwell, Dame Edith. *The Queens and the Hive*. Boston: Little, Brown, 1962.

"The World of Mary Queen of Scots." Marie Stuart Society, www.marie-stuart.co.uk/ (accessed November 18 2006).

Transcribing Elizabethan letters to Mary:

"Palaeography." National Archives, UK Government Records and Information Management, www.nationalarchives.gov.uk
palaeography/where_to_start.htm (accessed November 20, 2006).

The cipher used in the Babington Letters:

"Secrets & Spies." National Archives, UK Government Records and Information Management,
www.nationalarchives.gov.uk/spies/ciphers/default.htm (accessed May 31, 2007).

NAPOLEON BONEPARTE

Bryant, Mark. "The Scourge of Napoleon." *History Today*, August 2006, pp. 58–59.

Markham, J. David. *Napoleon for Dummies*. Hoboken, N.J.: For Dummies, 2005.

Markham, David, and Cameron Reilly. "Napoleon 101" podcast (accessed November 1, 2006).

Meyer, Arline. "Re-dressing Classical Statuary, the Eighteenth-Century 'Hand-in-Waistcoat' Portrait."
Art Bulletin, March 1995, p. 45.

Napoleon. DVD. PBS, 2000.

Napoleon: The Myth, the Battles, the Legend. DVD. Bfs Entertainment, 2001.

Steckel, Richard H. "Health and Nutrition in the Preindustrial Era: Insights from a Millennium of Average Heights in Northern
Europe." National Bureau of Economic Research, www.nber.org/papers/w8542 (accessed January 15, 2007).

PETER THE GREAT

Massie, Robert K. *Peter the Great: His Life and World*. New York: Knopf, 1980.

Peter the Great: The Tyrant Reformer. DVD. A&E Home Video, 2005.

Russia: Land of the Tsars. DVD. A&E Home Video, 2003.

RICHARD III

Brotton, Jerry. "Shakespeare the King Maker." *BBC History Magazine*, December 2006, pp. 45–47.

Richard III Society, www.richardiii.net (accessed December 17, 2006).

Richards, Jeffrey. "The Riddle of Richard III." *History Today* 33, no. 8 (August 1983): 18–25.

Weir, Alison. *The Princes in the Tower*. London: PIMLICO, 1992.

VLAD DRACULA & VAMPIRE LEGENDS

Ancient Mysteries: Vampires. DVD. A&E Television Networks, 1994.

Bloodlines: The Dracula Family Tree. DVD. A&E Television Networks, 2003.

Florescu, Radu, and Raymond McNally. *Dracula, Prince of Many Faces: His Life and His Times*. New York: Back Bay Books, 1989.

In Search of History: The Real Dracula. DVD. A&E Television Networks, 1998.

Mackenzie, Richard. "Vlad Tepes: Ruthless Ruler." *Renaissance Magazine* 11, no. 50 (2006): 34–35.